Who Is
Christ?

Who Is Christ?

Anthony Padovano

AVE MARIA PRESS
Notre Dame, Indiana 46556

First printing, 25,000, October 1967
Second printing, 25,000, February 1968
Third printing, 35,000, January 1969
Fourth printing, 15,000, February 1971
Fifth printing, 10,000, January 1972
Sixth printing, 10,000, January 1973

NIHIL OBSTAT:
    John L. Reedy, C.S.C.
    Censor Deputatus

IMPRIMATUR:
    ✝ **Most Rev. Leo A. Pursley, D.D.**
    Bishop of Ft. Wayne-South Bend

Copyright 1967 AVE MARIA PRESS

Printed in the United States of America.

The Author

Anthony T. Padovano was born in Harrison, New Jersey, in 1934 and attended Seton Hall University and the Immaculate Conception Seminary in Darlington. He received licentiate and doctorate degrees in sacred theology from the Gregorian University in Rome.

Father Padovano is presently professor of dogmatic theology at the Immaculate Conception Seminary, Darlington. He is a member of the Newark Archdiocesan Commission for Ecumenical Affairs, a member of the Commission for Instruction of Clergy in Documents of Vatican II, and an elected "delegate at large" of the Senate of Priests of the archdiocese. He also acts as a consultor to the National Catholic Office for Radio and Television.

Previous writings of Father Padovano include the book *The Estranged God* (Sheed & Ward, 1966) and various articles on scholarly and popular theological subjects in such magazines and journals as *Ave Maria, Guide,* the *Catholic World,* the *Christian Century,* and the *Homiletic and Pastoral Review.*

CONTENTS

Preface

Strange as it may seem, in this time of intense interest in the renewal of the life of the Church, the tremendous explosion of published materials has concentrated on many of the peripheral, although important, aspects. In our concern for the Church's reform in law and liturgy and in our impatience to involve Christians in the real questions facing mankind today, e.g., peace, hunger, overpopulation, race problems, war, we could be neglecting the core question: Who is Christ?

The *Ave Maria* magazine, a national Catholic weekly published at Notre Dame, Indiana, is particularly anxious that this question not be overlooked. The editors of *Ave Maria* recently recognized that much of the discussion of the problems facing the Church seemed impoverished and lacking in a specific contribution to an understanding of them. It was becoming apparent that Christians were leaning almost exclusively on motivation and sources that bypassed Christ and his message, motivation that was primarily inspired by a humanism that lacked vitality and strength.

It is our feeling that Christians have a specific contribution to make today in the dialogue for answers to human problems. But to witness to that contribution we must have a sure hold on our identity. That is why the question "Who is Christ?" is crucial.

This book grew out of the *Ave Maria*'s attempt to initiate discussion into this question. We turned to a young, creative theologian, Father Anthony T. Padovano, to provide some insights into the understanding of Christ and our identity as his followers. The results far surpassed our expectations. Both editors and readers were enriched by the experience of reacting to an original, thoughtful mind meditating on the central fibers of our commitment.

Introduction

To neglect Christ is to neglect history to some extent and human feeling in its deeper dimensions. No man in history has influenced more people, inspired more institutions, evoked more thought. No other has stirred such profound human feeling. Many have knelt before his cross in guilt or read his words in wonder. Many have known their keenest joy or found their deepest peace in the memory of his Resurrection or in the reenactment of his Last Supper.

There are few serious men who do not take Jesus Christ seriously. Those who take him most seriously are Christians. For Christians alone confess Jesus as Lord and Saviour. Those who do not go this far confess Jesus as unique and often enlist him in the cause of human betterment.

In this book, we shall try to answer a number of questions about Christ. We shall do this by asking questions both about him and about ourselves. Our approach will not be scientific. It shall be inquisitive, existential, reflective. Our object shall not be discovery but encounter. The urgency of the question "Who is Christ?" makes such a question unavoidable; the largeness of the question, however, makes it unanswerable. A full answer to Christ demands a full answer to God, history, life, and love. We have a final answer to none of these. Therefore we have no final word on Christ who touches all these realities.

In the following eight essays, we shall ask ourselves a number of questions which approach an answer even if they do not achieve one. Why is Christ elusive? Why is Christ critical when God seems distant? Why has the Council made the question of Christ more urgent? Why is a theology of failure part of our vocation to Christ? Why do we need a new ascetical theology and what form should it take? What does our present crisis tell us of Christ? How can we realize in our lives the meaning of the cross in an age of affluence and the reality of the Resurrection in an age of disbelief?

The disciples of the Lord experienced him in a new way when he once asked a question of them: "Who do men say I am?" If now we ask a question of the Master, if we wonder in this book, "Lord, who are you?" we do so not for further knowledge but for fuller experience of him.

Anthony T. Padovano
Immaculate Conception Seminary
Darlington, New Jersey

I

The Elusiveness of Christ

In this first essay, I would like to say something about the nature of the question "Who is Christ?" and something about the context in which I believe it ought to be asked and answered. These remarks may prove somewhat less concrete than those that follow them; this is due to the nature of our subject matter.

The question is simply too large a question for theology to answer. It is a community question which only the community and the theologian together can answer. We must, therefore, not allow only the theologian to speak. We must hear also the simple words of the uninstructed, the wise words of the pastor of souls, the confused words of someone locked in doubt, the persuasive words of the preacher of the Gospel, the authentic words of the teaching Church, the inspired words of Scripture, and even the silent words of those who have met Jesus in such exuberance that they have no words to say of him. We shall find Jesus only as we do all the things a Christian must do, and only after the whole community has been heard.

There has perhaps never been a time when the Christian community has failed to ask itself who Christ is. Nor has there ever been a time when the Church has been able to give itself a fully adequate answer. Why is this so? The elusiveness of a total answer concerning Christ is due to the nature of Christ and of his community. Christ is remarkably the One of whom we can ask questions everlastingly. This is so because he is not only Someone for the Christian community but also One who is becoming Someone for us. Christ manages to be Christ somewhat differently in successive moments of Christian history, and even at any one moment of history he is so rich a reality that he escapes our total comprehension. Not only is Christ ever becoming Someone for us but he becomes what he will in unexpected and unheard-of ways. There is a continuity about Jesus but not a predictable pattern.

When we say that Jesus is Lord of history, we imply that a full understanding of him requires more than an understanding of his own history. For Jesus is the Christ who is present not only in heaven or in his own history but in the life process of the Christian community. Thus, he becomes the one Christian absolute because he is never absolutely stationary. He alone can identify with the community's every moment of existence. Jesus is not only the same yesterday, today and forever but he is the same in different ways.

Even with ourselves we realize the truth of this affirmation. We remain the same even as we become different with certain people and at certain moments. The same-ness of being a person is the same-ness of changing constantly, yet changing in a way which never makes us completely someone else. It is this ability to have a history to ourselves, a beginning and an end, which makes us one even as we change and go on becoming "who we will be." The history of each one of us is always our history and not someone else's history: This is true because there is something about us which unites our past with our future and makes us someone in the present. Once we begin our life, we can never become someone else although we are always becoming "who we will be." This is the drama of being a person; it is a drama that we witness most clearly, perhaps, in the child who is someone now even while he is on the way to becoming someone in the future.

The whole meaning of a person is understandable only when a person has lived his full life and has meant all he is to mean for history. There is a time when the history of every person is a complete history, embracing the whole time during which a person went his way in freedom from birth to death. It is this fact of our becoming "who we will be" in history by means of our freedom which explains the mystery of the human person. We truly know who a person was only when a person's freedom has been exercised in the whole range of his history.

When we deal with Christ, we deal with Someone whose full history includes not only his historical life but also his continual presence to his community in the Spirit: Christ not only has a pre-Resurrection history, but he is the One and the only One who rises from the dead *in* history—therefore, he lives on *in* the community. In our dying, we pass from his visible community; our hope is not for resurrection *in* history but at the end of history. Jesus, however, is different. For, all that Christ is includes all he was in his own history and all he has become and will become for his community. The Resurrection, for example, must include not only the rising of Jesus from the dead but it must include all this meant for the community of Christ in all its moments of history. Only then can we fully understand what the Resurrection was.

This community, then, cannot live only in remembering what Christ was in the beginning; it must also discover what he is and what he will be in the present and the future. Therefore, we truly call this Jesus the Christ—the Messiah who has come and is here and who is yet to come—the Saviour who once redeemed and who is ever about the work of redemption and who has not yet redeemed fully. This is the Christ we make bold to question in this series, and whom we hope to hear in the answers we formulate.

I would like now to return to something I alluded to at the beginning of this essay. We must be careful, in seeking to understand Jesus, to utilize more than intellectual categories. What Jesus means to us cannot be conveyed only in concepts. Our religious problem today is not only a theological problem, it is often a psychological problem and a spiritual one. One does not discover Christ when he finds the right words and formulas. Moral behavior, psychological maturity, value systems—life itself—are all indispensable in the search for Christ. Concepts enhance these factors; they do not substitute for them. Thus it happens that sometimes a correct theology misses Jesus. Thus it happens that sometimes one meets Jesus with the wrong theology.

Thomas believes in the Risen Christ not when he is told that Jesus lives again but as he finds the Lord present before him. Mary, at the tomb, fails to find the Master's Risen Body and in this experience, without a word or even a concept, she understands Easter. We must never forget, then, that we are a community which has undergone the experience of Jesus and therefore speaks of him; we are not a community that thought of Jesus and then met him. This is why there can never be a philosophy of Jesus. There is a faith in Jesus, even perhaps theologies of Jesus. The faith of the Church, however, is greater than her theology: Theology's service to the Church is not in giving the Church her faith, but in finding adequate concepts and words to express a faith which is already there.

Why do we say this? We say this as a reminder that Christ is not one who must be made relevant to reason alone: He is relevant to the total experience of being human, to the suprarational experience of love, to the many-faceted experience of faith. Even the right theology avails little in the discovery of Jesus if one has not discovered him in that pre-theological situation we call faith. This is why it is so wrong for the community to look to the theologian for too much. A Christian must never turn to theology for his faith or his hope or his love. These are found only in Christ and only in one's association with his fellowmen.

Some become desperate in their search for the right theologian and the right book and the right theory. In so doing they forfeit the serenity which is God's gift to those who live by faith and who know deep in their hearts that no theology is fully adequate to faith or totally enduring. The search for a relevant theology must always proceed from the awareness that every theology is somewhat "irrelevant" to the full mystery of Jesus.

In this attempt to put theology in perspective, I do not wish to minimize the eminent place theology must be given in the Christian community. Theology is of critical importance for the community's comprehension of its mission and its message and its Master. Although it comes after the experience of Christ, it is not, for all this, unimportant.

When a man has properly verbalized and conceptualized or even theologized his experience, he has come into a fuller possession of what he is about. As we live, we do not want only to experience our life. We want to think about it and to speak about it. This thinking and speaking about our life are not an extra or a luxury: Those who do not think or speak of life miss something of the experience of living, for experience seeks expression and grows through it.

It is true, furthermore, that we are not always best qualified to express even our own experience. Thus we look to writers or poets or artists or musicians to express something of what we ourselves have undergone and to do it in a way we cannot. If society loses its artists it loses something of the experience of living; if the Christian community loses its theologians, it loses something of its total grasp on Christ.

Society, however, does not ask its artists how to live; it must live first before it can appreciate what its artists are saying. So the Christian community must not ask its theologians how to find Christ without either wanting to find him or having found him. If one is capable of understanding art he is better for it; if a Christian is capable of understanding theology, he is likewise better for it. Even on a more commonplace level, we realize how others can sometimes speak our experience better than ourselves. We have all had people tell us things about ourselves which we had experienced and yet were hardly aware of. Thus we say: "That's true. I never thought of it. But now that you mention it, I see the point." We know it is true because we felt this and now see the correctness of someone else's observation. We are better for having heard this of ourselves. Sometimes we even spontaneously ask someone else to help us understand our experience, as two people who undergo an experience together may ask each other: "What did you think of that?" They ask not only to learn what the other thought, but also to sharpen their own understanding of the situation.

The theologian, then, has an enormously important service to render to the Christian community. He must realize, however—and the community with him—that the words of a theologian can make theological sense only to those who live in the faith and experience of Jesus. When a theologian speaks to someone who has not met Jesus in this way, he speaks concepts and ideas but not theology; when he becomes himself a scientist or a thinker lost in the drift of his methodology, he ceases being a theologian. For a theologian must be a man of faith and prayer before he becomes a theologian. He must be a Christian as deeply as possible before he takes up the burden of helping Christians understand Christ.

Christians must never be afraid to speak of Jesus. If we fear too much the correctness and the "relevance" of everything we say, we shall either say nothing or speak artificially. We are a community which speaks of Christ even as it tries to speak correct concepts of Christ. Even Scripture looks to Tradition for clarity; even the theologian looks to the community for direction. While no one speaks of Jesus perfectly, all must seek to say something. Society does not allow only its artists to speak of life. Although theology is the effort we make to say as well as possible what must be said, it must not become the only thing we say. A theologian must listen to the community. He needs its speaking about Christ, for his own words are most apt when they are spoken in fidelity to the community's faith, in loyalty to Scripture, in the context of a Christian Tradition theology itself cannot comprehend. When theology is a true theology it speaks of Jesus more accurately than anything else available at *that* moment of history; yet even the truest theology cannot become authentic teaching or Scripture or Tradition.

The community, then, petitions the theologian to speak of Jesus just as someone less skillful with words may ask another to write about his love. The lover must be the judge of the adequacy of expression; he must not allow the words to become artificial words. Furthermore, the lover, however inarticulate he may be, must himself speak to his beloved not only the better words of another but also the stammerings and stutterings of his own passion. Both serve their purpose.

All must speak in the Church without fear or inferiority or embarrassment. Only if all speak and listen can the richness of the Spirit's charisms become incarnate in the community. As all speak we shall find Jesus together. We shall find Jesus not only as we read the theologians, but also as we hear Scripture and celebrate the sacraments and have a regard for each other. We shall find Jesus as we seek the courage of faith and the joyousness of prayer. We shall find Jesus in the humility of our hope and in the constancy of our love.

For Jesus is not an answer to a problem or a question. He is an answer to life and the sum total of everything it means to be a Christian and of everyone who is a Christian.

Questions for Further Discussion

1. Why cannot we give a fully adequate answer to the question "Who is Christ?"

2. What does the author mean by "Christian community"? What does this have to do with determining who Christ is?

3. Relate what the author says about person to the presence of Christ in history and in our experience of his presence.

4. Why is our religious problem today not only, and perhaps not primarily, a theological one? How can the theologian help us? The artist? Do we need other help also?

5. How would you formulate a definition of faith in terms of what the author treats in this chapter?

6. What does it mean "to speak of Jesus"? What relationship has this speaking to faith, experience, theology, community?

II
The Problem of God

We have arrived theologically at a time when our understanding of God and his meaning for us have become a central issue. It is fashionable today to be in the midst of a "search," to have a "God problem" or a "faith crisis."

I do not mean to underestimate the very real anguish we are going through and the very real difficulty we face. Sometimes, however, we talk ourselves into problems. Sometimes, too, the problem we have with God is really a problem with being patient with life and with ourselves. Many of us want the problem of God settled early in life so that we can know precisely where we are and exactly what to do with God. Not only do we want the problem solved early, but we also want it solved in a static and definitive manner. We do not want ever to have to rethink our attitude and idea of God—even though we rethink everything else as we go along in life.

At a time when our generation is questioning everything and is sure of very little, it gratifies me to know that we are having a problem with God; for this is a sign that our approach to God will not become disengaged from our approach to life. One wonders how "real" God can be if we never raise a question about him. God, after all, can survive our questioning.

One wonders, too, how much of a mystery God can be if we manage to solve the problem of God when we have not solved anything else in life. God, like life, is Someone we wrestle with. He is

Someone whose magnitude not only renders us serene; he baffles us and upsets us, refusing to allow us to have done with him in our facile solutions. He haunts us more than he dominates us; and he makes every one of us unsure about him at times. Who is the man who is fully sure of himself? Who is the man who is fully sure of his neighbor? Why does it surprise us, then, to find ourselves at times unsure of God? God is the One whose continual elusiveness makes us humble and grateful before him. He is the One whose unspeakable transcendence turns us to Christ for Someone to hold on to.

God is the One whose obscurity turns us to each other as we ponder and seek. It is the very "unclarity" and "unpredictability" of God which have made us a community searching together, a pilgrim people even with regard to God. Had God been simple and obvious to each of us, we might have grown distant from each other. The silence of God in history serves its purpose. It forces us to come to terms with each other and to take God seriously. For God is a venture man must always make, a venture with a purpose and a victory but a venture nonetheless. God's "unavailability" to us has done more than anything else to convince us of our humanity and of his "otherness."

A modern Christian, then, constantly mistrusts those who know all about God's existence or non-existence. The facile tell us God is alive and then proceed to explain exactly what this means. Or they tell us God is dead and then present this astoundingly simple solution as something we should have known all along. The God whose existence or nonexistence can so easily be explained is a God hardly worth bothering about. The people whom I have cared for most in life, and loved deepest, are those whom I could not describe in a superficial or undemanding manner. What an irony it would be if people were more difficult for me to understand than God!

For all of this, the problem of God always remains an unsatisfying problem for a Christian; the problem of Jesus fascinates him more. Methodology and the mood of our generation demand that I do what I am trying to do now; to speak first of the problem of God and then, later, of the problem of Jesus. When one forgets his methodology, however, he remembers that the only God he ever knew was the God Christ taught him to call "Father." I suspect that the next major development in theology will take place in Christology. The very ardor of our present effort with God will turn us more intensively to that Christ whom we call the only Way to God and his only Word. The present silence of God has created an advent of expectancy and a quiet excitement for His Word. Even in our own lives we know how interested we become in the silent who finally speak. One who talks continually is seldom heard; one who may speak or may not speak is someone we wish to hear.

The New Testament and the early Christian community quite clearly and unashamedly translated the problem of God into the problem of Jesus. The very centrality of Jesus in the Christian community's religious endeavor witnesses to his divinity or, to speak more biblically, to his unique Sonship with God. This transferral of the community's search for Yahweh into its concern with Jesus is much more amazing than we at first suspect. It was a daring and an ever-to-be-repeated solution. One must "forget" God except as he is seen in Christ if one intends to be Christian about his faith.

In this time, then, of the "distance" of God, of our radical incapacity to speak adequate language about God, in such a time, the clarity and concreteness of Christ make him the critical point in our discussion.

Are there some distinctive features of Christ which may aid us in our discovery of God? I would like to cite two characteristics; more are in order, but an exploration of them would prove unmanageable.

Christ reveals to us, first of all, a relationship of God to his community which we could not have suspected. That God should be interested in human community is surprising. That he should enact a sacred history in the midst of one human community is also unexpected. Christ, however, tells us something more. God is found *only* in community. There shall never be a discovery of God except by those who build human community. There shall, furthermore, never be an *explicit* discovery of Christ except by those in Christian community. God comes only to community-makers. This is startlingly proclaimed by Christ when he makes love of neighbor the measure of loving God.

Christ convinces us, furthermore, that God does not come to his community from the outside. Rather, God reveals himself in our togetherness, first of all, and then makes clear the durability and transcendent possibilities of our togetherness when rooted in him. A Christian, knowing that God dwells only in community, makes his search for God his search for his fellowmen. God, surprisingly, becomes more certain in those moments when we grow more certain of our meaning for each other.

Christ reveals even more: God's presence in our community is not elusive, for the Word has become flesh in our history and in our community. Thus God has become a very concrete problem; his presence has become a very definitive and a very irreversible presence. God's revelatory activity with us reveals fundamentally his place in our community. Thus, so long as a Christian remains in history, he always finds God: For God was also a moment in history. So long as a Christian remains in community, he always finds God: For God was once in visible community with us.

The search for God, as a Christian sees it, is also a search for the right community. The right community does not mean the right Church as much as it means the right kind of Church. It is not enough for the Church to profess the right faith; it must also create a community for the right type of love. For even faith is not an end in itself. Faith is for love, which is the only absolute. Thus, faith and hope do not prevail at the end of time. Love, however, is unconquerable. Faith and hope pass away but love is eternal with no beginning and no end. For love is the only value which is Person. A Christian knows, furthermore, that love is community (Trinity or creation or

Church). God is real only *in* a community, for a community is the only place where love and, therefore, God can happen.

The second of the characteristics I alluded to before is that Christ reveals to us not only the fact that God is always in community; he reveals to us also that the Word of God to man is Man. This means that God is found in our humanity, in our human-ness. We said before that God comes only to community-makers. We say now that God comes only to those who want to be human. Those who want to be human recognize the unspeakably profound depths of human living. Even God is not too much to find if one enters into the *full* experience of human living. Every man who truly seeks himself seeks Christ, and every man who seeks Christ finds God. (Conversely, all who find God seek Christ.) In addition to all the "other-ness" of God, there is a harmony about God and man in Christ. It is not enough to seek God. A Christian proclaims as history's supreme religious moment a Person who was as human as he was divine.

God comes to those, as we said before, who do not fear but who build community. God likewise comes to those who do not flee but who accept humanity. Being human is the most difficult and the most religious of all our undertakings, for being human means accepting the sacredness and fragility of one's own life. It means living every moment with tragedy at hand and grace close by. Being human means forever trying to settle oneself in all the unsettling situations of life. It means accepting the freedom and the unknowability of the human enterprise. It means that anything can happen to us. We can gain the world and lose God or forfeit life and find love. Being human means fear and loss, pain and the cross. It means hope that must go on in a resurrection we may doubt from a Christ who is no longer visible. Being human means reaching for the stars and the person next to us at the same time; it means also missing the stars and the person nearby.

To accept all the potential of human living is to open oneself to grace and to the possibility of God and to limitless horizons. Doubt and denial diminish us; they are often the sign of a narrow spirit, closed to the thrilling affirmations and incalculable options opened to those in faith. Denial is often a sign of surrender to problems and an acceptance of fatalism. Faith is for the creative, for the strong and the brave, for those who dream even a new earth and a new heaven, a new life and a new man. Faith is a refusal to allow anything to limit life, even death. A Christian believes that human life opens into divine life which knows no limit.

Human experience is so multifaceted that God spoke his final Word to us through it. Thus the problem of God begins and ends in a Word too human not to have been divine. The problem of God can be summed up in a Word we call Jesus and God calls Son.

Questions for Further Discussion

1. What is the most frequently expressed formulation of the so-called "God-problem" today? What would be a more forthright statement of it?

2. What purpose does the "silence of God" in history serve? Is the calm, unexamined life usually the most healthy one?

3. Explain what the author means by the statement that "God comes only to community-makers." How does God become "more certain in those moments when we grow more certain of our meaning for each other"?

4. What does it mean to fully accept our humanity, to be human, and what does this have to do with being close to God? Is this a different type of "spirituality" from that which was formerly counseled?

5. Does it take more or less faith to accept your own humanity and to work with it than to withdraw from it and the world in which it is immersed?

III
Christ in Dialogue

The Second Vatican Council made the question of Christ more urgent. A realization of this requires some awareness of the basic factors behind the entire conciliar experience. Two key principles did more, I believe, to shape and structure Vatican II than any others. In this essay, I would like to discuss the first of these, dialogue. Even a brief survey of the major Council documents shows the impact of this principle.

The Constitution on Revelation describes the basic structure of Christianity in dialogical terms: Christianity became a possibility because God did more than speak to us; he actually cared about our answer. Thus, Christianity is in tune with its fundamental constitution only when it allows the principle of dialogue to assert itself. God's Word establishes itself in reciprocity; God's Church finds itself in the same manner. Since reciprocity is an absolute demand upon persons, even in the Trinity, there can never be a person or a personal Word or a personal community without communication or dialogue. Persons come to be only in relationship to other persons. This is true of the Trinity and of us.

The Constitution on the Church proceeds along the same line. The Church achieves itself in relationships: with God, among all the members of the Church, with the rest of the world. There is no Church without a series of operative relationships, relationships which are always maintained and never resolved. The Church belongs to Christ because of its relationship to him; it is catholic or universal because of its ability to relate to all men.

The Constitution on the Church, therefore, is a charter for intramural dialogue. The scriptural image of the Church as the "people of God" is deftly explored to explain this. Dialogue is essential for the Church, and this necessity arises not only from the nature of God's Word but from the way it is addressed to us. For God speaks his Word only to the *whole* community. Thus no one person or one structure in the community receives the Word of God.

This radical equality in the reception of the Word of God does not mean that all receive the Word in *exactly* the same manner. If such were true, a community would not be necessary, charisms would be pointless and dialogue would really be monologue. When we say that God has spoken equally to the community, we mean that anyone anywhere may have heard the Word, and that only everyone everywhere functioning in community can declare the Word's total meaning for us.

What practical consequences does this ecclesiology have? The Council and the postconciliar period have delineated some of these. There must be constant dialogue within the Church. Pope and bishops must speak to each other (collegiality; the synod of bishops) not only for the good of the Church but for the discovery of their own function within the community. Bishops and priests must speak to each other (the diocesan senate).

Clergy and laity must speak to each other (the pastoral council). This dialogue is not done only for the sake of expediency; it is not done only because it leads to a more efficient, a more contemporary or a more democratic method of managerial procedure. This dialogue is demanded by the essential principles on which the Church is structured, and it is a very theological, a very traditional, a very apostolic method of community procedure—for only in proper dialogue can the Church realize itself.

The nature of this dialogue is so critical for the whole Christian effort that it must prevail even with the other Churches: *The Decree on Ecumenism* called for a dialogue with every person and every Church which bears the name Christian. This dialogue, like all dialogue, is meant not for dominion, but for unity and mutual enlightenment. It is a dialogue in which neither side wins but both sides gain. It is a dialogue yearning toward love and salvation, conducted in hope, tending toward a distant but brilliant vision. It is a daring dialogue begun by members of a family who know their common origin and sense their common destiny but who, on the way, have forgotten the right words and the right sentiments. It is a dialogue in which brothers seek their Father and seek each other. It is a dialogue which needs a new language, a new mentality, a new theology if it is to live. It is a dialogue which strives for all of this, and which knows it is worth it because we are about the work of building a new family. And we shall achieve this as long as we talk sincerely to each other.

The Council, therefore, calls us to a vast collaborative effort within both the Catholic and the Christian communities. It asks us, in effect, to banish fear, to break down barriers, to join hands and hearts, to speak to each other in ways we have never done before. In our isolation from each other, there is fear; in our coming together, there is hope; in our common mission, there is love. Too much is at stake for us not to take a risk with each other.

The Council, for all the eagerness of its call to dialogue, does not oversimplify the task: For dialogue is not mere chatter or cheap talk; it is an effort at love and at community. Thus the Council tells us that within the Catholic community genuine authority and ultimate decision-making by a few cannot be set aside. It tells us that within the Christian community a Catholic and a Protestant witness must find their place. These antinomic elements cannot be jetisoned; they must, however, realize themselves in terms of dialogue, mutual service and true community.

The Council requires more. We must talk sincerely not only to those within the Church but to all the human family. We must join with men of faith and religious communities wherever they are found (*Declaration on Non-Christian Religions*), for a Catholic senses kinship with all who give their devotion and their hearts to God. The Council asks us, furthermore, to dialogue with the world at large, to speak to men of no apparent faith, even to those whose hostility startles and frightens us (*Constitution on the Church in the Modern World*). The Council, in summary, asks us to respect all men of goodwill and to give every effort at good faith a hearing *(Declaration on Religious Freedom)*.

If we miss this principle of dialogue we have missed the whole point of Vatican II, for Vatican II did not teach only in its 16 documents; it taught, rather, in the experience and the struggle to communicate. To speak in the way we have been describing requires from us a new effort at asceticism, an asceticism which does not retreat into unthreatened isolation but which absorbs the shock, the confusion, the promise of dialogue. Such speaking is not for men of narrow vision or little faith or no confidence. Such speaking requires painful growth.

If we miss this principle of dialogue, we miss a precious opportunity to help and heal contemporary man. For modern man needs and wants community more than man has ever wanted community before. Community always happens when people appreciate each other and talk sincere words to each other; modern man is almost pathetic in his eagerness to talk, in his hunger for truth, in his yearning for acceptance. This need has been rendered more acute by a culture which calls us not to real dialogue but to a projection of the proper image. This need has been made more painful by the sense of insignificance we all feel in the magnitude, the complexity, the rapidity of contemporary life. We seek more ardently, therefore, another person's attention and acceptance. We seek each other and, therefore, we seek true community. It is the task of the Church to create just such a community for modern man.

I said earlier that the Council has given an increased urgency to the question of Christ. I would like to explain briefly why this is so, at least with regard to the principle of dialogue; I shall deal in the next essay with the urgency of Christ relative to a second conciliar principle.

It is only as we look to Christ that we understand the nature of a dialogue which is truly Christian, for the dialogue we speak of must not be pointless or aimless; it is about something, ultimately about Someone. It is not a dialogue which is only secular or humanitarian in its objective. It is a dialogue which *eventually* becomes explicitly sacred, salvific, religious, Christian. We speak ourselves in this dialogue and, since we are Christian, we *eventually* speak Christ. We speak Christ to our fellowmen not because we were told to, or out of compulsion, or for want of something else to say; we speak Christ from the conviction that there is nothing better to say and that there is nothing that modern man wants to hear more as he comes of age. There is simply no one who can help man more than Christ. After we have educated, housed, fed and celebrated modern man, someone has to tell him what he was for and why he was here. This is why we speak of Christ.

Since our conversation with modern man about Christ is not a monologue, we must take modern man where he is and not where we wish he were. Thus, we do not threaten him with Christ or overpower him with Christ or artificialize or anathematize him with Christ. We encounter him with Christ. For Christ is not a waste-maker who devastates those over whom he exercises dominion.

Christ is the One who called us no longer servants but friends. He is the One who wept for us outside Jerusalem, forgave us from the cross and promised us peace on Easter morning. Christ is the One who quite simply and quite unashamedly loved us. This is the message and the Person we preach.

As we take up the conciliar mandate for unrestrained and unrestricted dialogue, Christ becomes a more critical concern for us. Whether we speak to those within the Church or to those anonymously on their way to the Church, our approach is the same. We look to Christ and strive to emulate the characteristics of his dialogue with the human family. I would like now to cite three of these for consideration.

• God is the One who takes the initiative in the dialogue with man. If he does not speak, no one happens. He creates; he structures community; he offers friendship. When Christ enters into dialogue with us, he also takes the initiative. He comes into our history even though our history was not tending his way. He calls the Apostles and pronounces salvation. His openness is so radical that the cross becomes a possibility. His appeal to love is so intensive that it continues even after our total rejection of him, beyond death, into Resurrection. Such initiative is unheard of. It manifests superabundantly a forgiveness **more** than seventy times seven. Christ's initiative is everlasting, and it leaves us defenseless before it.

Our dialogue with our fellowmen requires such a perspective even though we cannot repeat it. It is our task to become those who constantly take the initiative and who pray that their courage and their hope will endure beyond rejection. Without the Risen Christ, we would not have known how limitless love can be, how tireless true love really is, how translucently brilliant a thing love can be when it expresses itself even unto death and beyond hatred.

A Christian is wise enough to know that true dialogue with the members of his own household is sometimes the most difficult dialogue of all, since it has for its purpose the fullest type of community possible. Christ would not have died unless he intended more than superficial community. Christian dialogue, then, is not only an attempt at self-fulfillment; it is also a painful process of self-surrender. The most frequent rejection comes from one's own; the most agonizing rejection comes from them as well. When one is rejected by one's own, he has nowhere else to turn. Christ is the One who came among his own and his own received him not. It was only as Christ lost his life for his community that new possibilities opened up for us. In asking us to do likewise, Christ has called on us to do too much. Therefore he promises us his Presence and his Spirit.

• A second characteristic of Christ's dialogue with us was its recognition of the law of gradual development. God did not do everything all at once for the Jewish community; Christ does not do everything all at once for the Christian community. Love cannot be accomplished in a moment— it grows, and it takes time. Sometimes we give the impression that the fullest expression of Christian love must occur right now, in this generation, before the decade is finished. Christian love, however, always has a task to do and a disappointment to be sustained. It is forever unfinished just as Christ is unfinished (as we mentioned in the first essay). Christ did not enact the Resurrection at Bethlehem, nor at Nazareth, nor even in his preaching: The Resurrection was the last step. Even then Christ assured us that another and radically different step would be taken in the Return.

As Christ exemplified the law of gradual development, he also made it clear that Christian love must always take place in a situation. Christian love is not an abstract love by which we love all men of all times all at once; rather, it is painfully concrete, which means that we love these men and this time, hoping for ever-greater love. There is no other time to love except this, our time. There are no other men available to my love except these men in my situation. If I fail to love in a situation, I fail utterly at love. Even Christ had only a certain moment and a certain number with whom he could only do so much. He did not spend his time wishing to have been alive at another time or in another place. He too resisted the temptation of thinking that love is easier elsewhere.

I said before that the step beyond the Resurrection is a radically different step. I say this because it is only in the Return that Love becomes a situationless love. In the Return and in the eschatological kingdom love shall be an all-time, undeveloping, absolutely universal love. Unfortunately, many of us expect the eschatological kingdom now and, therefore, become impatient with the slow, very concrete and quite restricted form love assumes now. This historical Jesus makes it clear, however, that human love only happens gradually.

• A final characteristic of Christ's dialogue with us is its accessibility to all men. This does not mean, as I said before, that we actually love all men; it means that we are ready to do this. Universal accessibility presupposes our having loved in the concrete. Christ accomplishes his mission specifically before he makes it available to all men. The Resurrection becomes a universal promise only after it achieves a specific expression. A Christian, then, loves the person nearby in order to love all who come into his life.

The universal accessibility of love is accomplished eventually in the Spirit of Jesus. When Jesus loved us, he loved so well in the concrete that his ability to love universally was believable. This utter universality of love means also that there is an exciting unpredictability about Christian love. For a Christian may love anyone at all, even unto death. True Christian love takes us on an uncharted course. All we know is *that* we shall love: Whom we shall love and how are not predetermined.

This unpredictable character of Christian love, this universal accessibility of Christian love, requires courage which few of us have and which all of us must pray for. It is taking up such a love, however, that can make of us martyrs or saints. We may sense, on the way, that we have failed so often that we question our Christian commitment. We may regret all life long that we have loved ourselves too much or too well. Yet Christians who look to Jesus for guidance in dialogue know that in all the unpredictability and failure of their lives they are about something significant. For one day Easter morning will happen to us and to all those we loved so tenderly that we could not bear to be without them.

Questions for Further Discussion

1. Christianity has a "dialogic" structure; that is, God has spoken to us and he expects a reply. What does this mean in terms of our speaking out in the Church today?

2. Read over again what the author says about the nature of dialogue. Of course, it is an ideal, but is it entirely unrealistic to hope for in the Church and the world? What is the alternative?

3. What has dialogue to do with community? How can dialogue include those outside the community, even the secular and atheist? Does this mean that they have something to add to the conversation?

4. What does the Resurrection have to do with the character of dialogue? What practical difference does the Resurrection make in your life?

5. What practical implications for your own life have the author's reflections on the concreteness and the gradual development of love, and on the unpredictability of Christian love?

IV
Christian Secularity:
A World Truly Worldly

I have suggested that there were two key principles operative at Vatican II which both shaped the Council and made the question of Christ more urgent. In the last essay, we explored the principle of dialogue. Here I would like to discuss a second critical principle: the principle of secularity. As with dialogue, we are concerned here with a principle which shall require of us a reshaping of our community.

A precise definition of secularity is both elusive and crucial; for if we exaggerate secularity we cease being distinctively Christian; if we ignore secularity we become progressively less catholic or universal. If dialogue depends upon the nature of God's Word and the way it is addressed to us, secularity depends upon the nature of the Incarnation and the manner of its historical contingency. If dialogue requires our talking to each other of Christ and community, secularity requires our recognition of this world, time and history. Dialogue issues from the very nature of God who communicates with himself in a trinitary expression; secularity issues from the nature of creation which God makes partly responsible for our origin and destiny. Dialogue looks to the words we speak to each other and our effort at mutual love; secularity looks to the world we live in and the human values we discover. Dialogue and secularity both strive to overcome fear: The former conquers our fear of each other, the latter our fear of our environment.

We have two tasks to accomplish before we speak of Christ and secularity. The first is to make a distinction between secularity and secularism; the second is to show how this principle of secularity was a key conciliar question.

The first of these two tasks is the easier. Secularism and secularity are distinguished from each other in somewhat the same manner as the world is different from Christ or as humanism is different from Christianity. Secularism is not wrong because it is untrue, but because it is not true enough. It absolutizes the contingent; it declares final the penultimate; it has no "beyond" about it. Secularism sees the world and time as all there is. Its hope is in its own mission and its own resources. It seeks an improvement of life as we find it. Though there is a nobility and a grace about secularism's call for improvement of life, the venture is perishable and finally futile. For life, no matter how improved it is, does not explain itself and is always taken away from us. Though there is a certain courage about secularism's willingness to bear bravely man's cruel situation, the approach has a fatalism, a fear, a tediousness about it. Life is simply too grand for human reason to grasp it or human potential to exhaust it. Secularism asks us not only to walk with darkness on every side, which we must all do, but also to walk *into* darkness, which many of us refuse to do.

Secularity is quite another thing. It begins, as secularism does, with a love of the world and a sense of the tragic. It knows that innocence does not survive untainted in this world and that the world crucifies sheer generosity when it encounters it. It knows that death brings us forever to tears and heartache. It knows all this and yet it loves the world. For the world was not only begun by God; it is graced by God and going to God. Secularity is sensitive to the joy and sorrow of the present but also to the everlasting possibilities of a future life. Secularity's view of history is so open-ended that it is able to accept an Incarnation and a Resurrection. It calls us not to less love for the world but to more love. For we love something in a durable manner and we love it unto its own salvation. Secularity respects all the genuine values of secularism, but it brings them to another dimension. Secularity is secularism with a sense of direction and an undying hope. It is a secularism which has seen a new horizon and found its heart. Secularity has discovered not only the world but a Creator and a Redeemer as well. It believes that human life is so precious that grace can happen to it and that history is so sacred that God can take his place in it. Secularity is what happens to secularism with the advent of Jesus Christ.

The second of the two tasks we set ourselves before discussing Christ is more difficult. Secularity, we suggest, was one of the key themes of Vatican II. It is more accurate to say that Christian secularity was expressed in the mood of the conciliar period rather than in a series of documents. Christian secularity was a factor making possible *The Constitution on the Church in the Mod-*

ern World, the first encyclical of Paul VI (*Ecclesiam Suam*), the papal pilgrimage to the United Nations, the Vatican pavilion at the New York World's Fair, the constant concern with world peace, economic justice, political community and dialogue with atheism. The Church, in all of this, made it clear that it was not the world's rival but its partner in a grand enterprise.

Pope Paul expressed this theme eloquently in a speech opening the second session of Vatican II (September 29, 1963). The words from this speech were inscribed at the entrance of the Vatican pavilion in New York:

Let the world know this: The Church looks at the world with profound understanding, with sincere admiration, and with the honest intention not of conquering it but of serving it, not of despising it but of appreciating it, not of condemning it but of strengthening it.

In *Ecclesiam Suam,* Paul writes: "The world cannot be saved from the outside." At another point in the encyclical, he comments: "All things human are our concern." In his speech at the United Nations he explains the reason for his presence: "We here celebrate the epilogue of a wearying pilgrimage in search of a conversation with the entire world."

The Constitution on the Church in the Modern World describes in elaborate detail the Church's regard for the world and for all genuine human values. The references to Christian secularity are so many that citing them would overburden this essay with quotations. This theme of secularity is calling us, as we said in the beginning, to a re-shaping of the community. Recognizing this, Pope Paul challenges us in his first encyclical not to bind ourselves "to ineffectual theories or hard and fast forms when these have lost their power to speak to men and move them."

I would like now to try to synthesize what is implied in Christian secularity, and perhaps the best way to do this is to enumerate what I believe are its key principles.

The first of these is a recognition of the fact that the world and created goods have a value in themselves apart from any *explicit* religious meaning we assign them. The world must declare its intrinsic goodness to us before we can decide what Christianity has to offer it. Even though the world has not a total goodness or a sufficient finality about it, it does have, in itself, an identifiable goodness.

To the extent that the world has its own value, to that extent it must be loved. It must be loved, as our fellowmen must be loved, not as means to God but in themselves. The world is too significant and people are too valuable for us to love them only as a means to something else, even if that something else is God. Christ in the New Testament loves the Apostles for what they are and not only as a way to love the Father; he asks us to love our fellowmen *and* God, not to love them as a means to God.

Even in our common experience of life we can see the truth of this affirmation. A mother must not love her child as a means to loving her husband, for the child has a lovable value in himself, a value so final that it cannot become a means to anyone else. A woman loves her husband *in* loving her child who pertains to both of them. It is loving the world and man for what they are, in themselves, which brings us to a love of God and self. A woman knows her child is not her husband. She does not substitute her child for her husband in giving her love to her child. A Christian knows the world is not God. He does not substitute the world for God, or love God any the less, because he gives his love to the world. The world and our fellowmen belong both to God and to us; this is true even though they pertain to God and to us in different ways.

A second principle we must insist upon is this: The world looks to man, not directly to God, for its development and fulfillment. For the world was not given to man only as a gift, but also as an obligation. The world was left unfinished so that man might share in creation, redeeming the world from chaos. As man assumes responsibility for the world he humanizes it, for the world has no freedom or consciousness except in man. It is through the world that man becomes all he must be; it is through man that the world finds its place before God.

Our third principle is an attempt to describe more clearly our relationship to God. Man, we suggest, must look to God for assistance in man's mission to the world. On this point, the biblical message is clear in both testaments: The world cannot be transformed without God. For without God, man takes the world into secularism where it does not achieve its freedom and direction; without God, man turns totally to the world. He does not take the world somewhere else, but seeks to become the world. Without God, man is not on pilgrimage—he has arrived. Man needs God, then, in his mission. For man is never fully man without God; without God he builds a world, Tower of Babel fashion, unto his glory and he builds from sin. Without God, man betrays and misleads the world. Christian secularity gives us at one and the same time an awesome sense of responsibility before the world and a humble heart before God.

What is Christian secularity trying to achieve? The answer to this question forms our fourth and final principle. The ultimate purpose of Christian secularity is a world which is both secular *and* Christian. Just as Christ makes us more human than we can ever be without him, so Christian secularity makes the world truly worldly. Christian secularity opens the world to transcendent possibilities and to everlasting significance. The objective of Christian secularity is the true worldliness of the world, a world responsive to, but not identified with, the Church. For the world must never become a Church: It must be what it was meant to be. If the world truly becomes itself, it finds God and welcomes Christ; and when it has done this, it has fulfilled its mission and completed its history. A world fully worldly and fully Christian is the new heaven and the new earth Scripture describes. Thus, Christian secularity builds for two mighty moments in mankind's history, the present moment of pilgrimage and the promised moment of homecoming. These two moments merge into each other: For the second moment is not another moment but a fulfillment of the first.

I would like to conclude this essay with a comment on the increased urgency that secularity brings to the Christ question. A Christian who goes forth to meet secular society on its own terms needs Christ desperately if he is going to be absorbed by the world. Christian secularity means that it is a Christian who becomes secular; it is a disciple of Christ who faces the world. Christian secularity does not permit us to do anything at all for the world; it demands that we have a purpose. One whose love for Christ is shallow and whose sense of mission is selfish finds the world too much for him. He does nothing for the world but allows the world to overcome him. In a secular environment, prayer—and especially reflective contemplation—takes on a greater importance. For one is now functioning in a culture which readily celebrates man and easily rejects Christ.

A disciple of Christ, therefore, brings the world Christianity and not merely another brand of humanism. He seeks to give the world its ultimate salvation in Christ. He comes to the world, therefore, with a set of principles which point beyond humanism. He bears Christ to the world not only for the sake of God who created the world for Christ, but also for the sake of the world which remains unintelligible, even to itself, without Christ.

Even though a Christian and a humanist do the same things at times, they do them for different reasons. In the final analysis, these different reasons make a difference. Even if all the values humanism strives for could be realized, a Christian would still have a task to perform. He would be happy with all humanism had accomplished, but he would still have a further function to perform. A Christian feels that humanism never does enough and that it might just possibly close man in upon himself. Christianity brings humanism a salvation from its own failures. It tells humanism that even if man is completely educated, nourished, housed and respected, even if all this is achieved, someone must go on to tell man what he is for and why he is here.

As before in our discussion of dialogue, so now in this question of secularity: A new asceticism is required of us, for we must learn how to renounce and to embrace the world simultaneously. It is easier to totally renounce or totally embrace. Doing both requires a participation in the death of Christ to the world and in the Resurrection of Christ for the world.

One must learn to love both the world and Christ. For Christ is the Christ who came into our world and is always found there.

Questions for Further Discussion

1. Distinguish the principle of "secularity" from secularism. Does this distinction help to clear up the confusion about whether to hate or love the world? How can we renounce and embrace the world simultaneously?

2. Why does the author say that secularity was one of the key themes of Vatican II? What was the Church's attitude, or seemed to be the Church's attitude, before the Council?

3. What does the author give as the key principles of secularity? What kind of "spirituality" does secularity seem to demand?

4. What is Christian secularity trying to achieve in the world and for the world? Can there be such a thing as a "holy worldliness"?

5. Explain why today's man of the world needs Christ. Why he cannot settle for a simple and uncritical "humanism."

V
A Theology of Failure

Thus far we have considered elements which are more or less objective in the Christ question. In four essays, we have explored Christ as becoming; the concreteness of Christ at a time when God seems distant; the increased urgency of Christ as a result of the conciliar emphasis on dialogue and secularity, respectively. I would like in the next three essays to consider elements which are more or less subjective: our acceptance of failure, our search for a new asceticism and the need for fidelity. These are all critical factors in the discovery of Christ. First I would like to sketch what we might call a theology of failure.

In spite of the fact that Christianity speaks of the cross, redemption and sin, we are unwilling to admit failure in our life. This is partly due to human nature's defensive mechanisms against its own inadequacies. It is also partly attributable to the successful image our culture demands of us. The problem with projecting the perfect image is manifold. First of all, it is simply not true—we are not always happy, optimistic, in command. Secondly, projecting the flawless image keeps us from reaching people, who feel we just would not understand them. And third, even if we could live a life with no conflict, suffering or mistakes, it would be a shallow existence; the man who is deep is the man who has failed and who has learned to live with his failure.

A Christian is someone who wants to give his

life seriously for a noble objective. If he does not wish this, he is not a Christian. Every human life given generously for a lofty ideal is filled with regret as well as with joy. One of the most difficult things to accept in such a life is our failure to have done with our lives what we longed to accomplish. In a sense, this is the one cross we want least of all, the cross we never expected, the cross which is hardest to bear. Such a cross is all the more painful for those who, in the name of the cross, were once sure their lives would make a great difference.

Men have always been troubled by the seeming failure of their lives. Modern man, even more, is distressed by this. He is haunted constantly by a desire to do and to be everything. He finds it unsettling to be only one thing, only some one in this modern age. So many possibilities are open to us that the choices become bewildering: When we do finally choose, we are not sure we have chosen rightly. We want to commit and uncommit ourselves to many things simultaneously. We suffer, as never before, from the sense of our limitations, from our finiteness. We forget so often that our every success has a trace of failure in it and that no one of our failures is complete failure. No one thing in our lives can undo completely the good we have done.

Life, we must be reminded, is a continual loss and not only a continual gain. We do not ascend toward God or another life in a straight line. We go forward in a roller-coaster fashion, always going somewhere but not directly and not in a predictable manner.

Each one of us, Christianity tells us, must die to himself a little in order to succeed with himself. Each one of us must learn to be humble of heart, to realize that no one of us has all the answers even to his own life. We depend upon each other for our happiness and for our salvation.

We have made a world, unfortunately, as we said before, where people feel comfortable only when speaking of their success. And yet our needs today are so great that we do not have words for them anymore. If we try in any way to express this need we fear being misunderstood or being taken advantage of.

We have made a world where people expect instant and constant happiness. Happiness, however, is only for those who do not expect it at every moment, who receive it as a gift, who know how to live without it at times.

We have made a world which tries to tell us, in effect, that one day, somehow, sorrow and heartache will be banished. A Christian knows that there will never be a time when we shall not have to face tragedy together. The Master was crucified and told us that what was done to him would be done to us. A Christian is someone tired of all the purveyors of cheap solutions and slick contentment. He is weary of all the small talk and insincerity on the fairground of life which tell him that life is a game and that one must pursue its advantages relentlessly.

We have made a world which gives us many reasons for being pessimistic and fatalistic. A Christian knows, however, that no one can give him a *reason* for living and hoping—he has to choose these things. At any moment, we can choose to give up, to despair, to grow cynical, to decide there is no use. But what does this solve and what does this make of us? Christians are those who had every reason to despair and chose not to. For there is simply too much light, too much love, too much goodness in life for anyone to give up.

A Christian knows that the present age is one in which it is easier to stay alive and harder to be a human being. It is an age which asks us to look at life and to give it no meaning at all. Yet a Christian knows that Jesus Christ saw a meaning even in his dying and in our rejection of him. A Christian may not have explanations; he is expected, however, to have courage and hope. If we face life properly, we shall not unravel it but we shall discover it has a terribly important meaning.

We need someone to tell us again that all of us are afraid, that all of us are burdened with the memory of some failure in our lives. Christ is not for the fearless but for those who must hear him say: "Do not be afraid."

So many of us are afraid today. In our fear we narrow the catholicity of the Church. We want a Church for only the conservatives or only the liberals, a Church for only the clergy or for only the laity, a Church for only those who think exactly as we do and who have become exactly what we are.

There is fear, in this time of change, that the Church may move too quickly or perhaps not quickly enough. There is fear among some that the Church may move so fast that there will not be a real place for them in the Church of the future. There is fear among others that the Church may move so slowly that they will be frustrated in their hopes. It is precisely because the Church is a community that she cannot be exactly the type of Church any one of us wants her to be. She must be one Church—with room for all. She must be Christ's Church, not ours. Thus she will always do things we do not fully expect. This is a time when it is not easy to stand by the side of Christ or to stand with the Church. Christ, however, is not for those who have no fear.

Christ is not for the perfect but for those who need his word of reassurance. Christ is not for those who are convinced of their greatness but for those, like Peter, who wonder why they lost heart and began to sink. Christ is for those who, like Magdalene, know what they are capable of and who try mightily to salvage a few sacred moments in a life of so many ambiguous years. Christ is for those who, like Paul, still tend toward the things destructive of their life and vocation.

So often we forget how much Christ felt his limitations:

"Will you also go away?"

"Jerusalem, what I could have done for you! Why did you not respond?"

"Father, I do not want to die this way. Must I?"

"When I come back, will there be any faith?"

We must learn anew the old lessons. Discipleship in Christ is even now a cross. We shall not easily forget the Resurrection since our recent theology has stressed this so much. What we forget more easily is the price one pays for the Risen Christ. We need hope not because we disbelieve Easter, but because we lose heart during the Calvary moments.

We Christians may be revolutionaries, but we die. We strive for holiness and we sin. We reach for the light but fear the darkness within us. We need someone to tell us again that getting through life meaningfully is not our starting point but an accomplishment more difficult than we at first suspect. We are those who might have become anything, but who need all our strength to remain one thing. It is frightening to know we can become only one person and that we have only one lifetime. It is frightening to know this, but it is also wisdom.

A modern Christian must rejoice over the small victories in his life. He must count to his credit the way he lives every day. He must learn to measure his life not by the infinite future but by the limited present. He must remember the past not in terms of what might have gone right but in terms of what *did* go right. He needs the Gospel message to remind him that his mission to the world begins with the management of his own life.

We must be reminded again that the New Testament speaks of no one other than Christ who lives life without mistakes. Our inability to believe or to hope or to love today is rooted in our failure to accept failure.

I would like to make one final point before concluding. One of our deepest fears today, one of the areas where we experience failure most, is in accepting the signs of the times. If the truth be told, all of us are a little uncertain as to where the Spirit is leading us today. The Spirit has asked us to walk a path we had not expected. The Spirit once asked Paul on the road to Damascus to walk another way and to bear with the blindness for a while. Like Paul, we must admit our confusion but walk humbly and trustfully into a future which is not as clear as we would like. Our hope is in God who never ultimately disappoints his children.

Our faith in God is not always the real issue today. The issue so often is our loss of faith in the present. There is a feeling among some that the really real was in the past or is coming in the future. We must affirm again our faith in the present Church which is the only Church we have. We are not, let us remember, the first to have felt a sense of emptiness at times in following Christ. The disciples on the evening of the crucifixion must have experienced a painful confusion. We tend, however, to romanticize their distress.

An unspoken loss of confidence in the Church is another one of our problems today. We fear that the Church may mislead, and so we hold back. In our uncertainty, we look for someone to blame for the way things have gone. We blame the old or the young, the theologians or the bishops, the liberals or the conservatives, the priests or the laity. And yet no one of us is fully guilty or fully blameless. We have no need for accusers or victims. We have, however, a terrible need for each other and for this community.

The present is still filled, for all its problems,

with limitless possibilities. It is easy to lose our heart and our nerve as the crises of a changing Church press in upon us. It is easy, but it is not necessary.

This time is one in which we can feel even more keenly the redeeming and healing grace of Christ. We know that our problems are not only with the times but with ourselves. It is our failure with ourselves which leads us to blame the times. Our devotion has too often been a divided devotion—a spoken or a promised devotion, but a devotion without performance. In all this, Christ must become more our Redeemer, saving us from the mistakes and disappointments of life. In the midst of the darkness and storm, it is easy to lose faith in the light. And yet it is precisely in the hour of suffering that we are nearest to Easter. Unfortunately, it is also the hour when we doubt the most. Easter seems much more possible on Palm Sunday than it does on Calvary.

Our faith tells us, however, that life never ends, that freedom is never taken away, that the Master is with us on the troubled waters. Our theology tells us that no life is all wrong or all right. Christianity asks us quite simply not to lose hope.

For God became a Father most of all to the prodigal son. Christ became a Good Shepherd most of all to the lost sheep. And the Holy Spirit was given to us not because we are strong, but precisely because we are weak.

Questions for Further Discussion

1. Why do so many of us fail to recognize the real meaning and utility of failure and crosses in our lives? What is the correct and balanced attitude toward failure?

2. What part does personal choice have to play in a world in which there will never be a time when we are completely happy or satisfied or fulfilled?

3. What can we learn from Christ about success and failure? What is the meaning of the Resurrection in this context?

4. What does the author mean by saying that where we experience failure most today is in accepting the signs of the times? Can we, should we, take heart in the fact that the Spirit has asked us in the Church today to walk a path we had not expected?

5. Why is there an "unspoken loss of confidence in the Church" today? What is the proper attitude for the Christian in this time of trial?

VI
Today's Spirituality
for Today's Apostle

One of the reasons Christ is not real enough for us in this postconciliar era is that we seek him with a preconciliar spirituality. This does not mean that preconciliar spirituality was wrong; it simply means that it was preconciliar.

If we now approach Christ with a different liturgy, a different ecclesiastical structure and a different theology, we must approach him also with a different spirituality. If there is no change at all in our spirituality, it will become increasingly irrelevant to our total lives as Christians. We desperately need a spirituality, but it must not take us from our other tasks as modern Christians.

In this essay, I would like to suggest a few ideas on a spirituality suitable for those engaged in apostolic work—whether priests, religious or laity. This essay is more an effort at tentative probing than a finished synthesis or a final judgment. It seeks to fuse into a harmony the stress on personal initiative and optimism which characterizes the postconciliar period with the studied discipline and caution of the preconciliar period. We must express in one spirituality our acceptance of the world and our difference from it, our willingness to trust ourselves more and our awareness of how easily we deceive ourselves.

It seems to me that a modern spirituality begins with activity. The most decisive of all our decisions in life is the vocational decision—so decisive, in fact, that it radically affects one's spirituality. A spiritual program requires an understanding of the personality of the individual and of the apostolic work about to be done. One must know how he intends to dispose of himself before God and how he is to make himself available to his neighbor before he can determine a suitable spirituality.

Perhaps the most orderly method of procedure is to discuss prayer in relation to activity, first of all, and then, later, asceticism in relation to activity.

A Christian must realize that it is not only in prayer, but in labor, activity and service to others that he gives glory to God and builds the kingdom. Our lives are substantially realized not in our prayer but in our vocational pursuits: It is in being a parent or a housewife or a priest or a doctor that one gives character and shape to his life.

One does not become a housewife in order to pray; one prays in order to be a good housewife. One does not become a priest in order to pray; one prays in order to be a good priest. One, furthermore, becomes a good housewife or a good priest or whatever one becomes not because being good at one thing, even the priesthood, is an end in itself. One becomes something (parent, priest, doctor) in order to express love in a concrete way. Though love is the only absolute, it is an absolute which demands concrete expression. We pray, not because we see prayer as a value alien to our vocational activity, but because prayer enables our love

61

to become even more intensive and more concrete.

Thus, one must be careful not to overemphasize prayer. Prayer is for human and Christian living. The prayer of Jesus is a prayer in tune with his mission. He spends a night in prayer because he will select the Apostles at dawn. He prays long hours on another evening because the cross is imminent. He prays before his miracles, when faith seems frail in others, for his disciples at the Last Supper. This same attitude toward prayer must prevail with us. The Judgment of which Jesus speaks is a judgment concerned with what we became for our fellowmen. It is a judgment about the success or failure of our concrete mission of love to our contemporaries. It does not speak of prayer.

The life of Jesus makes it clear that his prayer depends upon his mission, but it also makes clear that Christian mission cannot be fulfilled without prayer. The "Lord, teach us to pray" is a petition each one of us must formulate. The way we shall be taught, however, is in the context of our life situation.

Granted all this, we might appropriately ask ourselves why we pray. We pray, first of all, to discover Someone. We never discover another human person unless we seek him and address ourselves to him. When we address another in terms of placing ourselves at his disposal and sharing our life with him, we call him friend. This is what prayer seeks more than anything else. It is a search for God and a declaration of our availability to him. We pray so that our relationship to God might become one of friendship and sharing.

We pray most fundamentally for his Presence in our lives.

Though we seek the Presence of God most fundamentally, we do not seek it exclusively. If this were true, there would be no serious command to love others nor any religious significance to the vocation in life we choose. We seek the Presence of God as we go about the life task we are to perform. We seek his Presence not only because he is preeminently the One to be sought, but because his Presence alone gives our labor a durable meaning and a consecration.

In this conception of things, is there such a prayer as a prayer of pure praise to God? There is, but the object of the prayer is the discovery and celebration of Love. Prayer is always about something else. It is always about love, our celebration of Love in itself or a prayer that love might be realized in a particular vocational situation. Both are necessary.

It is only when we forget that prayer is about something else that it fails us. We have all met people who pray much but who are forbidding. This can happen when prayer is seen as an end in itself or when prayer is thought to have a value apart from that love which alone can change lives.

It is not only the choice of vocation but the moment when one lives that vocation which must determine our prayer. There cannot be an ahistorical spirituality univocally applicable to all ages, any more than there can be an avocational spirituality suitable to all walks of life. Even the same vocation has a different spirituality at different moments of history. Thus, a spirituality for the married today differs from that of the last century; a parish priest today has a different spirituality from that of the Curé of Ars.

Today there are a number of characteristics which typify our prayer. We are most instinctive to rapid, informal, sung, social, scriptural, interfaith prayer. Other ages would be dissatisfied with our emphasis on every one of these characteristics. Furthermore, prayer in an age of personalism will lead often to reflection on self, our work, other people. This is true prayer so long as such reflection is done against the norm of Christ.

One final aspect of prayer which must be emphasized is a type of contemplative prayer for the modern Christian. There are moments when we must simply be silent. Otherwise we lose a sense of gratitude for life and we forfeit an awareness of its grandeur. This contemplative prayer must be contemporary and vocational in its structure, but it must be there. A technological age has not learned the value of silence; the human personality, however, needs silence. Otherwise, it fills itself with noise rather than with meaning.

In all of this there is no substitution of activism for spirituality—nor is there any trace of what seems to me equally false, namely, a replacement of prayer with work so that prayer as such is unnecessary. What we are insisting on is a dynamic spirituality and on work as an incentive to prayer.

I would like now to say a few words about asceticism.

There is opportunity for self-surrender in our vocational pursuit. This must not be minimized but utilized in our spiritual striving. The arduousness of our labor is truly burdensome, truly crucifying. Sin has made this situation even more trying, for our toil now often appears vain. Man labors not only in a sense of accomplishment but with a fear that his life's work may be useless. Death hovers over not only man but over his work as well.

Man tries to achieve in his life's work what he tries to achieve in his prayer: a kingdom of love where men can be men and see themselves as children of God. We pray because we lack love and must petition Love for love. We labor with the hope that in a world lacking love a new heaven and a new earth may come into being.

The cross of work is summed up for a Christian in the Eucharist, where his time, bread and effort are made part of the dying of Jesus. The failure of a Christian's work is joined to the failure of the cross not because failure has a finality to it, but in the hope of redemption beyond failure and resurrection from it. A Christian brings to the Eucharist his realization that he has not accomplished with his work what he wanted. He brings to the Eucharist the consciousness that his life has not gone the way he once dreamed it would.

Christianity promises man the possibility that his work might proceed from grace rather than sin. It speaks to him not of hopelessness but of confidence in the ultimate intelligibility of his efforts. Christianity cannot transform the toilsome character of work; this is the task of technology. Christianity can, however, give work a meaning and direction which the secular world cannot provide.

What a Christian hopes to do by his labor is to redeem the world to some extent and build for a future which will be an eschatological future. He labors more in hope and love than in accomplishment. In so doing, he decides to stand for values which may not be realized in his lifetime or in the lifetime of mankind—yet they are values worth standing for and dying for. He knows that unless a man discovers a value worth dying for in his lifetime he never really lives. What must be demonstrated to our contemporaries is the fact that a Christian can labor in hope, grace and confidence and do more for the world and himself than one who works in despair, sin and a sense of uselessness. A Christian works with a sense of humility knowing that neither his generation, nor even all generations, can do it all.

I would like to offer a few possibilities now, keeping in mind that the asceticism I am suggesting is more demanding than a freely chosen but more arbitrary asceticism.

One commodity we treasure more today than ever before in history is time—our time is precious. Giving it constantly to others, refusing to run from them or to hoard time for ourselves, is more demanding than fasting or abstaining from food. For time freely given is not only a surrender of comfort but an opening to the unpredictability of human encounter. Since our time belongs to others they can more easily make demands on our patience, our talent, our serenity. Trying to give time generously to others involves more heartache and more self-sacrifice than anything I know.

A second contemporary form of asceticism is the continual effort at communication. This is a time when old and young, liberal and conservative, Protestant and Catholic, believer and atheist stand in close proximity and some disagreement from each other. The effort to understand and reach others is painful. It means exposure to value systems and insights which disturb us and force us to rethink and deepen or even change positions. Refusing to communicate is comfortable. Genuine communication takes more from us than the sacrifice of material things. In both cases—that of time and that of communication—it is not something we own or want, but our very selves which are at issue.

Our involvement with the world is another source of ascetical endeavor today. Living in the world as much as possible and yet refraining from those things which can undo our witness is more agonizing than running from the world. If one withdraws from the world, his life becomes easier. The most difficult undertaking of all is facing the world with a stubborn insistence that Christian values will not be compromised.

These are but some concrete examples of an asceticism which does not take us from work, an asceticism which is truly demanding, and yet one which heightens brotherly love. To give our time, to try to talk and understand, to go out and meet the world—all of this demands more heroism than we shall ever have. As one does this, as he faces a multiplicity of demands upon him, as he suffers from the insolubility of so many situations, as he does all this, he suffers in a creative and Christian manner. If one can bear with all this, with his own shortcomings and those of others, with the trials of marriage or religious life, if he can bear with all this in equanimity, he will become a disciplined and loving Christian.

Is there a place in all this for an asceticism freely chosen apart from one's vocational pursuits? Such an asceticism (e.g., fasting, abstaining, etc.) has a place, but its place is secondary. An asceticism freely chosen should be directed to a specific person or a concrete objective. It should throw us back into life even more, giving us new occasions for love, new opportunities for surrender of self.

The New Testament shows us a Christ who suffers most when he gives himself to people who do not understand or care, or who ultimately reject him. Christ does not speak of the pain which comes from his fasting, only of the pain which comes from the uncomprehending. His fasting is always a concrete effort (e.g., he fasts in the desert because he will soon begin his ministry; he exhorts to fasting when his disciples cannot cure a specific person).

Our discovery of Christ is bound up, then, with our choice of the appropriate vocation and of a prayer and asceticism which are suitable to that vocation. Vocation, prayer and asceticism must become ways of giving one's life for others. It is only as we do this that we imitate and discover Jesus Christ.

Questions for Further Discussion

1. What is the principal difference between a "pre-conciliar" spirituality and one that bears the mark of Vatican II? Why does the author say that a modern spirituality begins with activity?

2. What is the primary function of prayer in modern spirituality? Contrast that with the reasons why we actually do pray.

3. What has our particular "vocational decision" to do with the way we pray? What is the real meaning of vocation in life?

4. What are the characteristics that should typify our prayer today? Is there room for a kind of "contemplative" prayer?

5. Outline for yourself the marks of a modern asceticism. What place has work, family, the world of the secular in spiritual effort?

6. Discuss the possibilities of what the author calls an asceticism "more demanding than a freely chosen" one: the giving of our time to others, the continual effort at communication, involvement with the world.

VII
Fidelity and Crisis

This book has touched on many issues concerning the identification of Jesus. It has not explored the historical Jesus, exegeted the New Testament or evaluated magisterial Christology, though this is the way we often go about answering the question "Who is Christ?" It is a commendable method of procedure but it must never become an exclusive method of procedure: The discovery of Christ in our life is not the discovery of an accurate biography of Jesus. In fact, the history of Jesus is only the beginning of an encounter with him. Even the Apostles had to look beyond the historical Jesus to the mystery of the Spirit and the building of the Church before they understood what Christ had to mean for their lives.

I would suggest further that even the official teaching of the Church, even her sacramental life, is not enough for the discovery of Christ. The preaching of the Church and her sacramental liturgy are only the starting point. A starting point must be taken fully into account, but it demands that a point beyond itself be achieved. If the preaching and worship of the Church were enough, we would only have to pertain to the Church to be saved. Yet many who pertain to the visible Church and enter into her life realize they may not be saved. Though Christ is always Someone I miss without the Church, he is also Someone I must appropriate to myself before he can be a Redeemer for me.

There has been too much stress lately on the

objective dimension, on the correct dogmatic formulation of the God-problem or the Christ-question. It is more than an inadequate conceptualization of God or an insufficient history of Jesus which is at issue. Our present faith-concern is certainly a concern for precise language and valid data, but it must be even more a concern with the way we approach the problem and with the way we handle life.

A Christian virtue which, therefore, needs emphasis today is the virtue of fidelity. One of the most impressive qualities of Christ is his faithfulness or fidelity to what he promises to be for us. One of the most distinctive features of Christian discipleship is fidelity. Faithfulness obviously cannot be arbitrary faithfulness: One must decide what is worthy of lifelong commitment before he casts his lot. There are always values worth the giving of one's life—they are usually values which come only to those brave enough to risk a lifetime on them and constant enough to labor for their realization in spite of reverses. Lifelong commitment is demanded not only by the nature of the case but also because of the cultural situation in which we live. Our society has become so complex that more often than not a lifetime is needed to prepare and execute a meaningful service to others.

What are some of the values worth a lifetime? This essay can only answer that question in the abstract, since a concrete response must be made by each person individually. The answer, furthermore, must exclude those whose emotional problems or physical handicaps will no longer allow them to remain faithful to the full living out of their vocations. We are speaking here of those who could have been faithful but chose not to be, either because the task was difficult or because they questioned the very value of enduring commitment.

Someone who has not remained faithful throughout is someone whose witness to others is compromised. Words move us deeply only when we know that the speaker will live and die for them. Words are ineffective unless they are deepened by deeds. Words that change men's lives demand as their substantial deed the giving of one's life. Disciples of Jesus Christ, therefore, are those who must do more than proclaim him: They must also act the way he acted. For Jesus Christ was not only God's Word to us, but God's act and God's gesture on our behalf. No one ever becomes Christ's disciple unless he learns faithfulness—a faithfulness that Christ demonstrated even unto death—a fidelity so deep that it could remain steadfast even on the cross.

Of all the values worth lifelong commitment, I would like to discuss only one in the remainder of this essay: fidelity to that community we call the Church. I choose this value for consideration because such fidelity is questioned today and because I believe that Jesus Christ is simply not discoverable except in community.

More than any other human community, the Church requires of us a lifelong commitment. In any personal community, it is the realization that certain people are present and that they will always be there which reassures us. A community which is truly personal and not merely organizational, a community of witness rather than function, requires enduring presence. Such presence is necessary in order that the community become a fully personal community. Such presence is furthermore required for the person to benefit from the community's existence. In childhood, it was not only the presence of one's family which meant so much, but the fact that they would always be present which mattered. The people who influence our lives most radically are those who are there not only in the dramatic moments when we need them but in the mediocre moments when we hardly give them a thought. We follow Christ because we believe that he is not Christ for a moment but for our whole lives and for all time. He has made a lifelong commitment to us, one which survives our inability to think of him always, one which survives even our rejection of him.

The community which stands for Christ cannot always be a dramatic witness to him. It has, of course, its moments: the Apostles or Nicaea, Vatican II or John XXIII, Paul VI at the United Nations. These moments are dramatic, but the community which stands for Christ sometimes stumbles and stammers in its effort to express him. It is a community which mediates Christ to us less in the drama of its proclamation than in the persistency of it. It has its moments of silence, its moments of painful embarrassment to us, its moments when it speaks in almost a contradictory fashion. On the whole, however, those who love this Church know that Christ would have been lost to history had this community not been here.

Often we criticize the Church because she taught us that very message which serves not only as her glory but as a judgment of her. The Church, like all people whose lives we share, disappoints at times but not ultimately. So often, now, we call her a pilgrim Church, and this is what she is. Too often we become annoyed because the pilgrim Church we eagerly preach has not become the triumphalistic Church we categorically reject.

This community is now quite clearly in a state of crisis and I would like to say something about this. I do not think, first of all, that the crisis is a bad thing for the Church even though it is a painful thing. It is not a crisis which has no program or purpose. It is a crisis in which some of the most important values are at stake: freedom, personal initiative, ecumenism, Christian humanism, relevant worship, creative theological thinking and corporate community collaboration. It is a crisis, furthermore, in our time. This is important to keep in mind. We generally think that the crisis we are going through is the worst crisis of all. We think this because we never experience the pain of other crises. We only hear about them.

Another distinctive feature of this crisis is the fact that it is a crisis the Church brought upon herself. This time, there are no threats from the outside. This crisis the Church herself precipitated, and she did it in the name of the very Gospel she preaches. The heart of the crisis is the searching reexamination of the nature of Christian community which the Church is exploring.

Vatican II is an indication that the Church intends to become less a structure and more a community. Every community requires structure, but structure, unfortunately, can exist without community. What the institutional community we call the Church is now trying to do is to reverse the process which the preconciliar period engendered. This institutional community is now seeking to become less institution and more community. It is superficial to say that the institution must go. The issue is not destruction of institution; every community must live with some institutional structure. The issue is the place or importance, not the displacement, of institution. Institution serves community. Its service to community, furthermore, is a searching service, which means that sometimes the institution, by mistake or by plan, will forget its role. At those moments the community must remind the institution of its purpose. To expect, however, that the institution must be thrown out every time it makes a mistake is to be naive. It is an indication of that we are forgetting the human nature of the Church and overlooking the fact that community, too, is fallible in its striving. The tension between community and institution is a healthy tension as long as we realize that community is always the prior value.

The concern of the Church now must not be a concern about whether or not she is the right Church. The concern of the Church must be a concern about whether or not she can become the right kind of Church. Those of us who intend to stand with her know that she shall become just that, and we intend to stand with her all life long because she is worth our lives and because our lives are more meaningful with her.

In saying all I have said, in describing the fact that the crisis is one of growing, that the crisis is from within and that the central issue is community, in saying all this I am emphasizing the objective features of the crisis. They are features which are present regardless of what our own attitudes or hopes or fears might be.

I would like now to attempt a description of some of the more subjective aspects of the crisis. I would like to try to say something not about the way things are, but about the way people are feeling.

I think that some are troubled because they are trying to understand Catholic Christianity from the top down. What I mean by this is that many are trying to understand the Church first and then fit the meaning of their lives into it. I think that this is a time when we must look at the meaning of life first and then see whether this leads to the Church. In the past, one understood the structures around him and achieved his identity by a relationship to them. In the present, we are trying to understand ourselves apart from, within or even against the structures we find.

If one believes the value of Catholic Christianity, he does not fear the shift of emphasis. He is convinced that approaching the Church from the meaning of life is a good idea and a new opportunity. If we say that everything Catholic is necessary to explain life, we approach the problem in a manner which is not sufficiently modern. Thus, we can be troubled in spirit. A reverse approach is more helpful: The vast majority feel that life has a meaning. If life has a meaning, its meaning is dependent on a faith in something durable. A Christian is one who professes that only God is durable enough for faith and that only Jesus allows faith to have a sufficient humanity to it. A faith which is objectless is no faith at all. A faith which is godless is a faith in something or someone more durable than oneself but not ultimately durable. A faith without God does not discover the durable: It merely finds someone or something which endures some moments more than oneself. A faith which is Christless is a faith which verges on the ambiguous and drifts toward awesome aloofness. A faith in Jesus is a faith in community. Somehow or other, Jesus is never an idea or a man but always a community. The very idea of him, the very humanity of him, leads to a gathering of those who recognize him as Lord into a fellowship.

What we are really saying today when we say we are critically interested in God's existence, Christ's identity and the community's function is that we want to reexamine our lives and faith again from the bottom to the top, from the most fundamental realities of all (God, Christ, community) to the less fundamental though necessary developments (Scripture, sacrament, dogmatic formulations). Unless the most fundamental realities are true and real, the successive realities become artificial and mechanical. In our effort to put the Church on a new path, we are proceeding correctly. We are asking ourselves if what we are doing today is exactly what we should be doing to find God, celebrate Christ and create community. If not, then perhaps we have been committing the community to a concern with the discovery of those things the community was not meant for. It is the subordination of Scripture, sacrament, dogma, structure to God, Christ and community which alone can save us.

A second subjective characteristic of the present crisis is a fear that distinctive values may be lost to the Church in the process of restructuring. This is a sign of little faith in the Spirit or of too much faith in our own idea of what is vital to the Church. When all is said and done, those values which have made Christianity what it is will remain. There will always be Christ—for Christianity is, quite simply, Jesus. There will always be the Gospel. There will always be the sacraments. There will always be our togetherness in fraternity and in faith. These shall remain. Therefore, why do we fear? Are such values not enough for Christianity and for us?

This anxiety about losing essential values often leads us to regret our moment of history. How unworthy this is! This moment is ours. We owe the past a loyalty to the present since the past can live only in the present. We owe the future a loyalty to the present since the future can inherit only what we allow to live in the present. Fidelity to the present is the key to fidelity to the future. For the future does not happen. It is made. The future is built only by those faithful to the present.

A third subjective characteristic of the present crisis is the temptation to run away, either by dramatically and decisively leaving the Church or by withdrawal and reaction from within. Some were willing to accept a Church in its easier moments but cannot abide a community in crisis. In difficulty, many surrender. The difficulty of the moment is undeniable—one book, one talk, one article, one theologian cannot solve the present crisis for us. We must all live through this.

In staying and struggling, in faith and fidelity we shall make this community live and prevail. And we do this not for the sake of the community but for the sake of our fellowmen. Human history has known nothing better than this Church, in spite of all its shortcomings. And mankind has no firmer hope than the Christ-hope this Church enshrines and preaches. We do not want this to be a community only to the young, so we want these older to remain; for the witness of long years is a beautiful and tender part of life. It is a sign of a history of fidelity. We need the wisdom, experience and mellowness of age. We do not want this community, furthermore, to be a community without the young. The imagination, excitement and newness of youth make life livable again. The witness of a pledged fidelity, sworn when life is just beginning to assert itself, inspires every one of us.

If we walk away, Jesus dies. This is how it happened many years ago. Jesus died when he was deserted to the last man. If our Church comes apart, Christ will not long survive. Even the other Christian Churches need our witness for the full living out of Christianity.

In our fidelity, we shall build a Church more splendid than our dreams. And then we shall dream new dreams that will demand we make her better. In our fidelity, we shall build a Church, even from the ashes if the Spirit so compels. There is more significance in fidelity to this Church than in desertion from it. We harbor no fear of the outcome. For we build with Jesus nearby.

Before concluding this essay, I would like to cite some benefits which the present crisis has brought us. In spite of all our problems, many of us would not want to go back 10 years. They were good years, but these years have a different promise and another purpose.

The present moment in the Church has given many a sharper awareness of what faith is. We are seeing faith more perceptively not only as an assent to truth but as a relationship of persons. Faith engages man's mind, but it also seizes his heart and enlightens his life. We are more conscious today of how much the community is involved in every personal act of faith. Faith is very much a corporate witness. Faith, we know now, is something we live by rather than something we defend. It comes to us in our courage and in our hope, most of all in love. It lives side by side with doubt, but it manages constantly to overcome it. Faith is every man's effort to take a step beyond himself.

The present moment has allowed us, furthermore, to see ourselves and others in a moment of self-questioning. It has revealed to us more of ourselves and others than we could have known without crisis. There has been pain and confusion in this, but the pain is not pointless. The pain is the agony of the human situation and of this modern moment from which we refuse to insulate ourselves. The pain is the agony of growth. To refuse to suffer now is an option all can make, but not without the penalty of remaining underdeveloped. This moment of crisis is showing us more of what we are really like. It has put us, furthermore, in fuller contact with others.

The present moment in the Church has shaken free from us many of our old, inhibiting fears. On every side, our fear has diminished: fear of the world, fear of non-Catholics, fear of non-Christians. Our new fears are not inhibiting fears, but fears which precede growth and encounter. We are more willing now to face the other, howsoever different he be, knowing that there is always common ground and that Christianity is too dynamic to fail.

The present moment has brought to the Church an outburst of initiative and creativity. We have become spectators of all the excitement of change, participants in the marvel of becoming, witnesses to the irrepressible youthfulness of the Spirit. As we go about our daily tasks, new ideas and new possibilities surround us. This institution is wildly and joyously alive. Nothing seems to be aging in it. It is not, of course, without its inner darkness—but it is reaching for a greater light.

The present moment, finally, has emphasized the irreplaceable and singular witness of each person's faith. All must stand up and be counted, not because we revel in numbers but because every charism of faith has something different about it. This crisis has brought us to face life at its most fundamental level so that we might go beneath our surface differences and surface fears to the heart of the matter.

The present moment of the Church is one in which it is trying to tell the world of its love affair. It is hesitant, shy, uncertain, but it is anxious to tell the world that the Church is hopelessly in love with the world. It is seeking to love first in the hope that the world will discover in its heart a love for God and Christ which it did not know was there. The present moment has its cross, but the cross has never been an end in itself. The present moment may not be a moment of arrival, but a moment of striving that seems more characteristic of a pilgrim Church. This moment of crisis is meant for togetherness. It is a moment to see Jesus in a new way. It is a moment of love. Hence, it is Christ's moment. Christians are those who promise never to refuse love or to deny Christ his moment.

Questions for Further Discussion

1. Why does the author suggest that it is necessary to look beyond the historical Christ and to have more than the official teaching of the Church, her preaching and sacramental liturgy for the discovery of Christ?

2. Why is fidelity or lifelong commitment a necessary ingredient of the Christian disciple today? Outline for yourself the reasons why the Church, in spite of her many faults, is worth this lifelong commitment.

3. Do we risk discovering Jesus Christ when we abandon the Church, the community which stands for him? Why should we not lose faith in the Church in the state of crisis in which she is today?

4. Why does the author say that Vatican II "is an indication that the Church intends to become less a structure and more a community"? Discuss the implications in the statement that "this is a time when we must look at the meaning of life first and then see whether this leads to the Church."

5. Why does the author say that today in the Church we must subordinate Scripture, sacrament, dogma and structure to God, Christ and community?

6. What are some of the benefits of the crisis of the present moment in the Church?

VIII
The Crucified and Risen Christ

In this final essay, I would like to say a few words about our search for an absolute value in life as well as something about the inner meaning of the Last Supper, the cross and Easter. The first of these points, namely, searching for an absolute value, may seem more abstract than it actually is. It is a consideration, however, which will enable us to understand better the points I shall develop after it.

Perhaps we can begin by reminding ourselves that the search for Christ does not always begin as a search for a determined person. The search for Christ is really every man's search for an absolute value in life. Christians identify Christ as the absolute value. Others either do not go that far or choose another path. For them, the absolute value may be Krishna or Buddha, Yahweh or Allah, classless society or human freedom. The search is real. It is universal and it almost always discovers something. This yearning for an absolute value is inseparably part of the mystery of human living.

When one explores in depth this agony for an absolute value, he realizes that we are not searching for *any* kind of absolute. We are searching for more than a value which explains reality. We are searching really for a value which explains *us*. This is why absolute values which are not Christ seem so insufficient to a Christian. Man's search for the absolute includes the hope that the absolute will be both personal and communicative. If the absolute is impersonal or silent, we are for-lorn. Christ is so absolutely meaningful for a Christian because he is so absolutely personal and communicative.

In reaching for the absolute, man seeks to find a personal value. Nothing disrupts human free-dom more than the choice of the impersonal. Nothing bewilders human consciousness more than the fear that at the end of it all there is only impersonality. An absolute which is im-personal is less absolute than the person who seeks it.

The search for an absolute, furthermore, is not only a search for an ultimate Person. It is also a search for complete communication. The absolute Person must speak an absolute Word to us. Otherwise we cannot be reassured or saved. We hunger after meaning. We strain to hear a Word which can explain us and declare us acceptable. If the absolute value in life cannot communicate with us, life has gone nowhere. For life is a search to speak ourselves and to hear another. How empty it all would be if we finally spoke ourselves to Someone who neither comprehended nor answered! What we yearn for at the end of our voyage through time is the discovery of a Word truly final, a Word that can bind together all our broken syllables and make sense of them. We want so much a Word which can heal our scat-tered phrases with harmony, a Word that can speak meaning into all the gaps and awkward si-lences of our life. The final Word for man will only be final if it sums him up and images God si-multaneously. If the Word can only speak of God or only of ourselves, we have traveled in vain. If the Word can only speak a partial meaning, then there is no hope for man. Our history has heard already all the contingent words there are. We need something more. Someone, somewhere, somehow must know what life is all about and must tell man this in a Word which makes ultimate sense. If there is no one who knows or if the One who knows will not speak his Word to us, then we are lost indeed.

There is something redeeming in the Word even before it takes on flesh. For the Word means that God speaks and that absolute communication has happened somewhere, at least once. Christ assures us that God's Word is not for God alone but for us. Christ tells us that we are anxious for communication because we have been made in the image of a God who sought and found forever an expression of himself and an answer from someone. It is God's ability to speak such a Word which makes him God. It is God's ability to offer such a Word which makes him a God worth seeking and a saving God. Jesus tells us that God's only Word is Love. This is why we are defenseless before God and why God is so irresistible. God has spoken the only Word man really wants to hear.

What Jesus had to say to us about God's Word was said most tenderly in his death and Resurrection. More than anything else, these two events have made Christ unforgettable. Thus when we remember him it is always in the context of his death and Resurrection through the signs of the Last Supper. The remarkable thing about the

Last Supper was not only Christ's wish that we remember him this way but the eagerness of the Apostles to thus remember him. Somehow or other what Christ had to tell the Apostles and what he had to be for them was experienced uniquely in that final Supper. If a moment for remembering had to be designated, this was such a moment. St. John tells us that Jesus spoke long and eloquently of love on that last evening. He chose this occasion to pronounce that one commandment Christianity was commissioned to proclaim. Jesus too was obedient to this commandment, an obedience which demanded from him the courage of the cross and the power of the Resurrection.

When the Apostles repeated the Last Supper, they did more than remember Jesus as he was then. They recalled him not only as the Master of the repast but as the crucified and Risen Christ. Their memory of him included now more than an image of the Rabbi who called them no longer servants but friends. It included also the image of the suffering Messiah and the victorious Lord of history.

There was something else about that Supper which made it so striking a way to remember Jesus. This Supper was clearly a mystery in which everyone present actively shared. Things were different on Calvary and at Easter. In those events, Christ seems alone, almost remote. He does things on Calvary and at Easter which he must do by himself even though he does them for us. At the Last Supper, this is not the case. Here nothing can happen without *us*. This is clearly an effort together. We share the meal together, hear his words of love, receive the washing of the feet, and partake of bread and wine. Jesus seems to die alone and to rise alone. He does not take his final meal alone. In the Supper, we are made aware of the community dimensions of the cross and Resurrection. Here Jesus reveals that the pouring out of his heart, the sacrifice of his body, and the shedding of blood are for this new community, this little flock gathered in the Upper Room.

Though the Last Supper is so filled with meaning, it must look beyond itself. The words and signs of the Supper are fully intelligible only after the cross and the Resurrection. Though the Supper is decisive revelation, it is not definitive revelation. The sacrificial dimensions of that last meal together are not clear until the cross. Nor is it yet sufficiently clear that this fraternal and sacrificial gesture is true celebration. This is not a memorial or a funeral banquet. It is a celebration of the glory of the Risen Christ yet to come.

The answer then to our recurring question "Who is Christ?" presupposes a word about the crucifixion and the Resurrection.

We can begin by asking ourselves what meaning the cross has for an age of affluence. I do not think that the fundamental message of the cross is suffering. The suffering of the cross is not meant for itself but for something else. Christ does not suffer because suffering is in itself a value but because love without restraint requires suffering. It is not a love for suffering which Christ reveals but a love which prevails in suffering. It is not the physical death of Jesus which is redemptive but the love of Jesus for us even unto death.

Traditional theology tells us Jesus need not have died to save us. It assures us that God could have saved us in many ways. It is not enough then to say that Jesus died for our salvation unless by this we understand something deeper. It is love alone which is redemptive. This is why God could have saved us in many ways. He could not have saved us, however, unless he loved us.

What, then, is the meaning of the dying of Jesus? Why could he not have loved us and redeemed us without death? The death of Jesus reveals to us how absolute God's love is. God's love is conditionless, expressing itself even to the point of ultimate donation in death. We were saved not by the physical death of Jesus but by the absoluteness of a love which did not count death too high a price. In dying, Jesus obeyed the Father's command that he love to the uttermost, that he love without any conditions. Such a love is so demanding that even the man Jesus must pray in Gethsemane for strength.

The dying of Jesus reveals to us not only how absolute God's Love is but also how communicative God's Love is. The death of Jesus is an act of communion, responsive to the Father and bestowed upon us. God's Love takes its place in our history and is shared with us in a unique way as Christ breathes his last. In the broken body of the Lord, the selflessness of God's Word and the communicativeness of God's Love are made clear.

If the fundamental message of the cross is not suffering but absolute and communicative love, then the cross speaks compellingly to an age of affluence. It reminds us that Christianity is not a choice of suffering or of deprivation but the choice of a new type of love. The love of Jesus is redemptive in its absoluteness and victoriously communicative in the Resurrection.

No matter how "advanced" or affluent we may be, love will always be asked of us. The cross reveals that the love demanded of us is an absolute and a sacrificial love. This love is absolute toward God and neighbor and sacrificial in both cases. Jesus loves the Father with an unfailing love and loves us to the point of death. He gives both the Father and us all his love. In each case, he sacrifices himself without restraint. What the cross makes clear is something we should have known all along, namely, that love is only real when it is absolute and sacrificial. Yet the cross reveals something we could never have suspected, namely, that God loves absolutely and sacrificially. It tells us, furthermore, that we are worth God's absolute love and sacrifice. This is unheard of, humbling, and gratifying all at once.

Even had sin never happened, love would still have been absolute and sacrificial in its demands. In the world we have made, however, love encounters suffering and death in its effort at absoluteness and sacrifice. Thus the agony and death of the cross became part of the revelation of Jesus to us. In the death of Jesus, we see the love he was trying to express. In our world, love is only absolutely believable when it does not count the cost of pain and the loss of this life. Thus the cross is both a revelation to us of absolute love and a sign or "proof" which makes such love believable. As Jesus breathes his last, he speaks a silent word of total love and offers his life in proof of this.

The final point I wish to develop concerns the Resurrection. What is most surprising about the Easter Event is the elusiveness of the Risen Christ. The Risen Christ is not as available to us as the crucified Jesus. Something new has happened. During his public ministry, Jesus gave us signs and wonders and asked for belief in them if we could not believe him. The time after Easter, however, is no time for miracles. The Christ of the Paschal Event requires a more intensive interiority in faith before he can be recognized. Now he does not speak of signs or wonders but tells us that Easter is meant for those who have not seen and yet believed. One cannot, of course, draw the line too sharply between the Jesus of signs and wonders and the Christ who is only available to our faith. It is the same Messiah of whom we speak. Yet we must remember that Jesus did not complete his history with preaching or miracles. These marked the beginning of his time with us. The last act of Jesus was a demand for faith in his Easter glory and the promise of a peace the world cannot give.

There is no area in the public life of Christ which has less a history to it than the Resurrection. This may mean that the substantial history of the Resurrection requires not only the activity of Christ in rising but also our faith and hope in this mystery. If the death of Jesus is a revelation of love in another dimension, the Resurrection is a summons to deeper faith and stronger hope. The elusiveness of the Risen Master is not arbitrary. It is an elusiveness for the sake of faith and hope.

Of all the things Jesus did, his rising is least real to history and most real to faith. This is not to say that there is *no* history to the Resurrection. Every Christian realizes that his faith is a faith in a history, the history of God's action in the Old Testament and of God's Son in the New. A Christian knows too that all our hope depends on the Risen Christ. If Easter is not history, then we must become cynics. For if Easter did not happen, we say in effect that complete innocence cannot prevail and that a Man who went about doing good was utterly destroyed by the mystery of iniquity. If that Man whose love and availability to others is celebrated by all men as unique, if he was conquered by the world and death and hatred, what hope is there for us who love far less than he did? If love, when it achieves absolute expression, as it does in Jesus, if such love can be crucified and silenced, if it can be buried with no further history, then we are doomed. Unless Jesus is risen, our faith is a faith in failure and our hope is a hope in a history which has no final victory.

The crucified Jesus is a sign that Christian love lives in a threatened situation. He shows us that if we accept all the consequences of love, love may suffer but it overcomes. The Risen Christ reveals that Christian faith and hope live also in a threatened situation. History tells us little of the Resurrection. Even Jesus is elusive after Resurrection. The crucified Jesus is real to those who accept an absolute demand upon their love. The Risen

Christ is real to those who accept an absolute demand upon their faith and hope.

Faith and hope in the Risen Christ become most radiant in the darkness when the star no longer sheds its light. It was in the midst of the deepest distress that the Apostles beheld the Christ of Easter. Just as the love of Jesus was revealed in his death, so the faith and hope he demands are revealed in his Resurrection. Such faith and hope have no natural explanation, no philosophical justification, no sign or wonder adequate to the task. Such faith is for those who hope beyond hope in a love that cannot die. The man of faith experiences the fragility of his resources and the threatening situation in which his hope must affirm itself. Yet he knows that in the midst of all the reasons and arguments against the Resurrection the Risen Christ appears. The man of faith has found a hope stronger than history and a love mightier than death. When he speaks of this, he does so haltingly. Yet those who stand with him in faith are the hopeful and the believers in love who know that if Jesus is not risen, there is no truth worth knowing.

With these final thoughts, we conclude our essays on "Who is Christ?" This series of essays sought an answer to an unanswerable question. It sought an answer by touching upon elements crucial to the discovery of Christ. We saw how elusive Christ is and how much he is a becoming reality. We saw how the problem of God made the figure of Christ more haunting and how the Council really summoned us to Christ as it spoke of dialogue and secularity. So often we suggested,

Christ becomes distant because we deny our failures and, therefore, do not seek him as Redeemer.
We observed that a more adequate spirituality
and fidelity in crisis are critical to an affirmation
of Christ. Finally, we spoke of our yearning for a
saving Word which loves us and for a Person
worth faith and strong enough for hope. In the
process of human history, God has enacted a great
sign. He has declared his love for us in Christ. He
has, furthermore, manifested his power in an
Easter Event that is the ultimate challenge to all
human faith and the invitation to final hope.

This book could not speak of Christ well even if
there were further chapters. In speaking inade-
quately of Christ, a Christian knows that he can
do no better. Yet he does not despair. For those
who hope in Christ believe also that one day there
shall be another time and another kingdom when
we shall say it all.

Questions for Further Discussion

1. Why is Christ the perfect answer, but one difficult of attainment, to the search for an absolute in life? What difference does Christ mean in your life?

2. What is the meaning of Christ's death and Resurrection for people today? What is the meaning of the cross in an age of affluence?

3. Why does the author say that the fundamental message of the cross is not suffering but "absolute and communicative love"? How, then, should we look at our own sufferings?

4. Why is Easter preeminently the feast of faith and hope?

5. After reading this book, what is your answer to the question: "Who is Christ?"